I know this to be true

NELSON MANDELA
FOUNDATION
Living the legacy

Ruth Bader Ginsburg

I know this to be true

on equality,
determination
& service

Interview and photography

Geoff Blackwell

CHRONICLE BOOKS
SAN FRANCISCO

in association with

Blackwell&Ruth.

Dedicated to the legacy
and memory of
Nelson Mandela

'My dream for the world is that we will all be better off when women and men are truly partners in society at every level.'

Introduction

When Ruth Bader Ginsburg started Harvard Law School in 1956, she was one of nine women in a class of five hundred men. Only one of the teaching buildings had a women's bathroom. There was no legislation preventing discrimination in the US, and some law firms wouldn't even interview women for jobs. It was a different time. Things were tough. But Ginsburg wasn't swayed.

Fourteen months after her first child was born, she began her legal studies. She didn't need a career of her own – her husband, Marty Ginsburg, was earning a law degree and could look forward to a well-paid job – but she valued independence. A desire for autonomy stemmed from her mother, who passed away when Ruth was a teenager. 'In those ancient days, most parents of girls wanted them to find Prince Charming and live happily ever after. But my mother wanted me to fend for myself.'[1] Taking her mother's advice, she set about forging her own path in life.

During the Red Scare of the 1950s,[i] at a time when many in the US were in the grip of fear and suspicion, she began to consider a career in law. 'I became interested in the law and in doing something to keep our country in tune with its most basic values – like the right to think, speak and write as one believes.'[2] This interest was developed even further in the early sixties, during time spent writing a book on Sweden's judicial system. There, the idea that men were the breadwinners and women the housewives – an idea prevalent in the US – no longer held sway. Journalists for major publications wrote about gender equality as an ideal; an article in the *Stockholm Daily* questioned why, when both partners had full-time jobs, the woman was still expected to take care of the children, cook dinner and clean the house. In Sweden, Ginsburg came to see the law as a means to advance the equal citizenship stature of men and women.

A guiding belief in the ideal of equality has framed her life and work. Ending gender discrimination has remained a core focus; in 1970 she co-founded the first US law journal focused solely on women's rights, later co-authoring the first law school casebook about sex discrimination and the law. In 1971

she co-founded the American Civil Liberties
Union's (ACLU) Women's Rights Project, which
aimed to end gender-based discrimination in
the nation's laws. As director of the project
she argued six cases before the Supreme
Court over a five-year period and won five.
When she became Columbia University Law
School's first tenured woman in 1972, she
stood as proof of the possibilities wrought by
the burgeoning women's movement.

Albeit slowly, things were changing.
During Ginsburg's time at the ACLU, the office
received a gradual flow of complaints from
women, ranging from those who couldn't
receive health insurance for their family
when a man in the same position could, to a
female tennis player who comfortably beat
her male opponents but was not permitted
to join the varsity team. 'People were lodging
complaints they were either too timid to
make before or were sure they would lose.
But in the seventies they could become
winners because there was a spirit in the
land, a growing understanding that the way
things had been was not right and should
be changed.'[3]

The road to progress wasn't smooth. Throughout her many years of tireless work Ginsburg has faced bigotry time and again. As a twenty-one-year-old working at Oklahoma's Social Security Administration she was demoted because she was pregnant when her employment commenced. (A decade later when she became pregnant again while working at Rutgers Law School, she wore her mother-in-law's clothing to hide the pregnancy.) On securing her first position as a professor in 1963, she was told by the Dean that, because her husband had a good job, she would earn less than her male colleagues. And in the early days of her career, she was refused positions as a law clerk because of her gender. When she asked one of the judges why, he told her working face to face with a woman would make him uncomfortable.

Yet rather than being disheartened by the setbacks she encountered, Ginsburg viewed them as opportunities to inform and enlighten. Some people just didn't understand why it was wrong to shield women from work as a lawyer, police officer, airplane pilot, and other fields of human endeavor. 'As an advocate in gender discrimination cases in the seventies, I thought of myself as akin to a grade school teacher. . . . The idea was to educate. The people I'm addressing don't understand, so I'm going to help them to comprehend what it is like, what life is like for people who are different.'[4] Minds could be informed, opinions changed, and progress achieved.

When she was appointed a judge of the US Court of Appeals for the District of Columbia Circuit in 1980, and then an Associate Justice of the US Supreme Court in 1993, Ginsburg was able to continue her important work. With a career spanning nearly six decades, she has dedicated her life to achieving equality. And in an age where it is desperately needed, she remains a stalwart supporter of justice and a reminder of the power of hope. 'The progress has been enormous, and that is what makes me hopeful for the future. The signs are all around us.'[5]

'It takes not only talent, but willingness to work hard, to make dreams come true.'

Prologue

From "University of Buffalo Honorary Degree Remarks", 26 August 2019

It was beyond my wildest imagination that I would one day become the 'Notorious RBG'. I am now eighty-six, yet people of all ages want to take their picture with me. Amazing!

If I am notorious, it is because I had the good fortune to be alive and a lawyer in the late 1960s. Then, and continuing through the 1970s, for the first time in history, it became possible to urge before courts, successfully, that equal justice under law required all arms of government to regard women as persons equal in stature to men.

In my college years, 1950 to 1954, it was widely thought that women were not suited for many of life's occupations – lawyering and bartending, military service, foreign service, driving trucks, piloting planes, policing, serving on juries, to take just a few of many examples that now seem senseless.

It was exhilarating to help bring down the barriers that, in Justice Brennan's words, put women less 'on a pedestal', than 'in a cage'.[6] So much has changed for the better since then. True, we have not reached nirvana, but the progress I have seen in my lifetime makes me optimistic for the future.

Our communities, nation, and world will be increasingly improved as women achieve their rightful place in all fields of human endeavour.

At a reception some years ago, a college student asked if I could help her with an assignment. She had one question and hoped to compose a paper by asking diverse people to respond. What, she asked, did I think was the largest problem for the twenty-first century. My mind raced passed privacy concerns in the electronic age, terrorist threats, deadly weapons, fierce partisan divisions in our legislatures and polity. I thought of Thurgood Marshall's[ii] praise of the evolution of our Constitution's opening words, 'We, the people', to embrace once excluded, ignored, or undervalued people – people held in human bondage, Native Americans, women, even men who owned no real property.[7] I thought next of our nation's motto, *E pluribus unum*: of many, one. The challenge is to make or keep our communities places where we can tolerate, even celebrate, our differences, while pulling together for the common good. 'Of many, one' is the main aspiration, I believe; it is my hope for our country and world.

'At many turns in my life, I have asked myself, "Is this something I really want?" And if it is, I find a way to do it.'

The Interview

Currently, and for the past twenty-six years,
I have been a member of the Supreme Court
of the United States. Before that I was a
lawyer and a law teacher. I had the great good
fortune to be around in the 1970s when, for
the first time in the history of the United
States, it became possible to bring down
the barriers that stopped women from doing
whatever their God-given talent enabled them
to do. In that decade, I litigated many cases
involving gender-based discrimination. In 1980,
I was appointed to the US Court of Appeals
for the District of Columbia Circuit, where
I served for thirteen years before my 1993
appointment to the Supreme Court of the
United States.

When I attended law school, women were
not more than three per cent of the lawyers
in the USA. My entering law school class had
some five hundred students; only nine of

them were women. That was an increase from my husband's class – he was a year ahead of me – in his class there were only five women. We had debated between business school and law school, and chose law school because the Harvard Business School did not admit women in the 1950s. I am heartened by the changes I have seen. Now, women are about half of law school attendees in the United States. Tremendous progress has been made.

You met your husband at university?

We met as undergraduates at Cornell University [in New York]. He was eighteen, I was seventeen.

And he was a feminist when you met him?

The word wasn't in common use in those days, but he certainly was. As I have said many times, he was the first boy I dated who cared that I had a brain. For a long time, we were best friends. We had been married for fifty-six years when he died. He was always my biggest booster. My biggest supporter.

If you were to reflect on your extraordinary
career and life, what has really mattered to you?

I had the opportunity to be part of a
movement for change, so that daughters
would be cherished as much as sons, and
women could achieve whatever their talent
and hard work enabled them to achieve.
There should be no artificial barriers, no
spaces women can't enter. There were many
closed doors in my growing-up years. There
was a time when women were not accepted
as members of the bar. There were no women
judges. Very few women engineers. No
women police officers. No women firefighters.
No women pilots of planes. Those barriers
are now, thank goodness, gone, and women
can do whatever their talent enables them
to do. Of course, it takes not only talent, but
willingness to work hard, to make dreams
come true.

'I'm satisfied when I feel I've done my job, when I've written an opinion that is as good as I can make it.'

What were your aspirations as a young person?

I was inspired by two females growing up.
One was a real woman; she was Amelia Earhart,
a great aviator when women were not flying
planes.[iii] The other was a fictional character,
Nancy Drew. In a series of books, Nancy was the
detective, and a leader.[iv] Her boyfriend followed
her around. She was a doer. In contrast, most
children's books when I was young portrayed
girls in pink dresses, not climbing trees.

At what point did you decide you wanted to
become a lawyer, and what was the motivation?

I decided to become a lawyer in the 1950s
when I was a college student. It was a bad
time for the United States. There was a huge
red scare in the country. An outspoken senator
from Wisconsin – Joe (Joseph) McCarthy –
saw a Communist on every corner.[v]
People were hauled before the house Un-
American Activities Committee[vi] and Senate
investigating committees,[vii] and asked about
organizations to which they belonged in the
1930s in the height of the Depression.

My professor of Constitutional Law impressed upon me that lawyers were standing up for these people – people accused of being disloyal – and reminding our Congress that we have a First Amendment that protects our right to think, speak and write as we believe, not as 'big brother' government tells us is the right way to think, speak and write. Lawyers were reminding the members of our Congress of the right to freedom of thought and expression, and that people have a right to be shielded against self-incrimination. They can't be forced to speak and, in effect, condemn themselves.

So that gave me the idea that being a lawyer was a pretty nifty thing to do. I thought I could earn a living, and also engage in activities to make things a little better in my society. I didn't appreciate fully the barriers to getting a job in the law. I did very well in law school, but not a single law firm in the City of New York would offer me a job. I had three strikes against me. One is I am Jewish, and anti-Semitism was a barrier. Second, I was a woman. Those barriers were *just* beginning to fall. The third one was a strike-out – I was a mother. My daughter was four years old when I graduated from law school. So the rare firms that would take a chance on a woman would not risk hiring a mother.

What was the narrative in those days? That you couldn't possibly juggle the responsibilities of motherhood and those of your profession?

I went to a university – Cornell University – when the Arts College had a ratio of four men to every woman. Parents of girls in those days thought the most important degree for their daughters was not a Bachelor of Arts or Sciences, it was the "MRS degree".[viii] My mother was not that way. One of the things she urged strongly was that I be independent. Her message was, it's fine if you meet Prince Charming and marry, but always be able to fend for yourself. Be independent.

Was your mother independent?

No, she wasn't. She graduated from high school when she was fifteen and went immediately to work to help support her large family so that the eldest son could go to university. In those days, if anyone was educated in the family, it was the eldest son. My mother was super-smart, and I think would have had a more satisfying life if she had continued working after she married.

Did she have the same work ethic as you?

Yes, she was very strict with me in that respect. One of my fondest memories is of my mother reading to me at a very young age. I would sit on her lap and she would read books to me – she was a voracious reader herself – that's when I began to love books. She would take me to the library once a week, I would wander through the children's section, find five books to bring home for that week, returning them the following week. It was a great sadness in my young life that she died the day before I graduated from high school. She battled cancer for four years, and then finally succumbed.

'My mother told me to be a lady. And for her, that meant be your own person, be independent.'

Tell me a little more about her.

Two things were important to my mother. One was that I be independent, and the other – she called it – 'being a lady'. And by that she didn't mean wearing white gloves. She meant that a lady doesn't give way to emotions that sap energy and do no good. Anger. Jealousy. Remorse. Those are emotions that don't move you forward, they trap you. So 'being a lady' meant don't snap back in anger, take a few deep breaths and respond in a way that helps educate people who don't understand.

My mother-in-law, on my wedding day, gave me the best advice ever. I was married in her home, and just before the ceremony she said, 'Dear, I would like to tell you the secret of a happy marriage.' 'Well, I'd be glad to have it. What is it?' She said, 'Sometimes it helps to be a little deaf.' That is, if an unkind or thoughtless word is spoken, tune out. I have followed that advice assiduously in every workplace, even to this day in my current job on the US Supreme Court. If an unkind or thoughtless word is said, just tune out. Don't let it get you down.

Where does this discipline and this drive
come from?

In part from some very good advice my father-
in-law gave me. I had two years between
college and law school, because my husband
was called into service from 1954 to 1956.
During those two years I became pregnant,
and worried whether I would be able to
manage a young child and Harvard Law School.
My husband's father said to me, 'Ruth, if you
don't want to go to law school, no one will
think less of you. You have a very good reason
not to enrol. But if you really want to be a
lawyer, you will stop feeling sorry for yourself,
you will pick yourself up, and you will find a
way.' That advice I have recalled at every turn
in my life. I've asked, 'Do I really want this?'
If the answer's yes, I will find a way.

Was it always so clear-cut being able to see
what you wanted and go after it?

When the women's movement came alive in
the late 1960s, I knew that's what I wanted
to devote my energy to. There were things

I had observed growing up, but as a young adult, I thought, 'Well, that's just part of the territory. You have to put up with it.' But in the late sixties, women began to think, 'No, we don't have to put up with it. We should be able to do whatever we have the talent to do. And no one should stop us simply because we're women.' Notably, there were several cases in which I represented men.

The way life was divided, and this was reflected in the law books, men were supposed to be the breadwinners, the supporters of the family. Women were to stay at home, taking care of the home and raising the children.

One example is a man among my favourite clients, Stephen Wiesenfeld. His wife died in childbirth, leaving him the sole surviving parent. If a male worker died, there were childcare benefits for the widow. But if a female worker died, there were no childcare benefits for the widower. That was wrong. And it stemmed from dividing the world into separate spheres: women and children go together, men work outside the home. We were trying to change that way of thinking so that men – if they were parents – would have the same benefits as women. And women who wanted to be whatever – a doctor or a lawyer, police officer or pilot – that would be fine.

Is there any advice you would give to prospective young leaders in parts of the world where gender equality is still a big issue?

If you want your country to succeed, you should put your money with the women. I think it's been shown that when women go into small businesses, and borrow money to do so, they're a more reliable credit risk than men in comparable situations. Given the chance, they will do the best they can, and they will pay it back. That's why I say if I were interested in development, I would put my money on women.

What have been your daily rituals as you've gone through your life and career?

I have one discipline – it started in 1999. It was the year I had colon cancer. I had surgery, chemotherapy, radiation, and my husband said when treatments ended,

"[W]e should not be held back from pursuing our full talents, from contributing what we could contribute to the society, because we fit into a certain mold, because we belong to a group that historically has been the object of discrimination."

'You look like a survivor of a concentration camp. You need to do something to build up your strength.' So I began working out with my personal trainer in 1999, and he is with me to this very day. He's written a book about what we do. It's called *The RBG Workout.*[8] Sometimes I become hugely absorbed in the work I'm doing and don't want to let go. But if it's time to meet my personal trainer, I just stop wherever I am. And I always feel much better when our hour is finished.

And you're still doing it?

Oh yes! Just yesterday.

In terms of your work, have there been processes or disciplines you've always applied?

When I was trying to achieve something much larger than myself, I knew I wanted to do the very best I could. When I first got into the business of striving for gender equality, most men thought there really is no such thing as discrimination against women. All the barriers were regarded as protections. So if women couldn't be police officers, it was because that was a tough job. If they couldn't be prosecutors, it was because they couldn't deal with the tough criminal types.

That excuse always surprised me, because women doing legal aid were representing these 'tough criminal types', and they had a much closer relationship with them than the prosecutor. Another example: Women didn't serve on juries because they were considered the centre of home and family life. What that says to a woman is, 'You're not *really* a full citizen.' Citizens have obligations as well as rights; men have to serve, like it or not. But the women are expendable.

I knew what I was doing was important, and that I had to make people understand how women were subordinated. People knew that race discrimination was odious, discrimination based on religion was a bad thing, but the barriers women faced – they thought they operated benignly in the woman's favour. So the job was to open their eyes to women's situations. As one of our Supreme Court Justices, Justice Brennan,

'Don't take no for an answer,
but also don't react in anger.'

put it so well, the woman was not, in fact, on a pedestal, she was, instead, in a cage.[9] A cage that confined her.

And you were, fortunately, well supported by your husband.

In every way. He was, as I said, my biggest booster. He also had a particular skill; he was a great cook. Our arrangement when my children were young, I was the everyday cook, he was the weekend and company cook. My daughter, in her teens, noticed the enormous difference between Daddy's cooking and Mommy's, and decided that Daddy shouldn't just be the weekend cook, he should be the everyday cook as well. So for all the years I've lived in Washington, D.C. – that's since 1980 – I've not cooked a meal. Since my husband died, my daughter – who is a very good cook; she learned from her father – comes once a month, cooks for me, and fills the freezer with food that I enjoy for the next month.

Was your cooking really that bad, or did your
daughter understand your mission as well?

My husband says he attributed his skill
in the kitchen to two women, his mother
and his wife . . . and I think he wasn't fair
to his mother. He said that he didn't know
the difference between chicken and veal in
his growing-up years.

Could you describe a key moment or crisis in your
life where your leadership has been truly tested?

I would say the biggest challenge for me
was ten years ago when my husband died.
But the next day there was a Court session
and opinions were to be announced. I came
to Court, I announced my opinion, because
I knew that's what he would expect me to do.
I feel his loss every day, but I think he would
be pleased about what I am doing.

Can you help young people understand how
you coped with that moment of crisis, how you
managed that grief?

I think, 'What would he have wanted?'
He would have wanted me to carry on with
my life, to thrive in what I'm doing. So I think
I honour his memory best by not giving way to
sorrow, but just doing my job as best as I can.

The stories you've told about your husband
are inspiring. Where did this generosity of spirit
and wisdom come from?

He was a very funny man. He had a great
sense of humour. I think he was so secure in
what he was, so confident of his own talents
that he never regarded me as any kind of
a threat, or competition. Just the opposite.
I think he believed that because he wanted
to spend the rest of his life with me, I had to
be somebody special. That was his attitude.

'I had the great fortune to marry a man who thought my work was as important as his.'

And he was kind.

Yes.

Tell me about how you've dealt with mistakes you've made, or where you've failed?

That's a question I'm often asked in the form of 'Is there any decision you made on the court that you regret?' My answer conveys some very good advice I received from a senior colleague when I was on the Court of Appeals for the D.C. Circuit. He said, 'Ruth, these are challenging cases; you're going to do the best you can with each one. But when it's over and done, and the opinion is released, don't look back. Don't worry about things you can't change. Go on to the next case, and give it your all.'

That counsel about looking forward, and not back, I think is very good advice for a judge. You do the best you can, but don't worry over what has been published and can't be changed. Just look forward and do the best you can in the next case, and the next case.

And lessons you've learned?

I believe that if at once you don't succeed,
you try and try again. You keep trying.

What do you think the world needs more of?

If I could pick one word, it would be listening
to others. Listening. Today, people tend to talk
only to like-minded people. I think social media
intensifies that tendency. I'm thinking of my
senior colleague, John Paul Stevens, who just
died.[ix] He was a great listener, and he spoke
about how he learned from listening, listening
to his colleagues who had a different point
of view. That is a serious concern nowadays.
People don't listen to people who have
different views; they just stick together with
people who believe the same things they do.
    But one of the things that has made
America great is its diverse population. So
many different backgrounds, racial, national,
religious. One should not just tolerate,
but even applaud our differences, and yet
join hands for the long haul. The motto
of the United States is *E pluribus unum*,

'Out of many, one'. We are one nation with a democracy I hope we can keep.

In your work you've had to be a listener, particularly in your role now.

Yes, it's a big part of the job. Listening to lawyers who argue before the court, listening to my colleagues when we confer.

What advice would you give your twenty-year-old self?

The first advice I would give to a girl just like me would be, 'Go for it.' You can make your dreams come true if you're willing to put in the hard work that takes. Something else I would say, whatever you do, whatever line of work you choose, always do something outside yourself. You're a member of a community, you are blessed with having certain talents. You should use your education and your talent to help make things a little better for people who are not as fortunate as you are.

Would you give any different advice for a
twenty-year-old boy?

As far as giving back to the community, no.
No I wouldn't. To a boy I would say, don't miss
out on the joys and the burdens of raising
your children.

'Fight for the things you care about, but do it in a way that will lead others to join you.'

Epilogue

*From "Remarks at the New York
Historical Society", 10 April 2018*

A French observer of early America, Alexis de Tocqueville, wrote that the greatness of America lies not in being more enlightened than other nations, but rather in our ability to repair our faults.[x]

Through amendments to our Constitution and court decisions applying those amendments, we abolished slavery, prohibited racial discrimination, and recognized men and women as people of equal citizenship stature.

Though we have made huge progress, the work of perfection is scarcely done. Many stains remain in this rich land. Nearly a quarter of our children live in poverty. Nearly half of our citizens do not vote. And we still struggle to achieve greater understanding and appreciation of each other across racial, religious and socio-economic lines.

We sing of America, "sweet land of liberty". Newcomers to our shores . . . came here, from the earliest days of our nation to today, seeking liberty, freedom from oppression, freedom from want, freedom to be you and me.

A great American jurist, Judge Learned Hand,[xi] understood liberty. He explained in

1944 what liberty meant to him when he greeted a large assemblage of new Americans gathered in New York City's Central Park, to swear allegiance . . . to the United States. These are Judge Hand's words:

> *Just what is this sacred liberty that must lie in the hearts of men and women? It is not the rootless, unbridled will, it is not freedom to do as one likes. I cannot define the spirit of liberty, I can only tell you my own faith. The spirit of liberty is the spirit which is not too sure that it is right. The spirit of liberty is the spirit which seeks to understand the minds of other men and women. The spirit of liberty is the spirit which weight their interests alongside its own, without bias.*[10]

May the spirit of liberty, as Judge Hand explained it, be your beacon. May you have the conscience and the courage to act in accord with that high ideal, as you play your part in helping to achieve a more perfect union.

'Work for what you believe in, but pick your battles, and don't burn your bridges. Don't be afraid to take charge, think about what you want, then do the work, but then enjoy what makes you happy, bring along your crew, have a sense of humour.'

From Notorious RBG: The Life and Times of Ruth Bader Ginsburg *by Irin Carmon and Shana Knizhnik*

About Ruth Bader Ginsburg

Ruth Bader Ginsburg is an American jurist, lawyer and Associate Justice of the US Supreme Court.

Ginsburg was born Joan Ruth Bader on 15 March 1933, in Brooklyn, New York, USA. Her mother was also born in New York, to Austrian Jewish parents, and her father was a Jewish immigrant from Ukraine. As a child, Ginsburg learned the tenets of Jewish faith. Her mother, to whom she was close, was a major influence in her life and impressed upon Ginsburg the value of independence and a good education. Sadly, she passed away the day before her daughter's graduation after struggling with cancer throughout Ginsburg's high school years.

At seventeen, she met then eighteen-year-old Martin D. Ginsburg while studying for a Bachelor of Arts degree at Cornell University in New York. They married in 1954 and she gave birth to their daughter, Jane, a year later. Fourteen months after Jane's birth, Ginsburg enrolled at Harvard Law School in Cambridge, Massachusetts, USA, where she was one of nine women in a class of five hundred men. Two years into her studies she transferred to New York's Columbia Law School, where she graduated with a Bachelor of Laws degree, tying for first place in her class.

Ginsburg struggled to find work in the legal field because of her religion and gender, and because she was a mother. Turning to academia, she became a professor, teaching civil procedure, conflict of laws, and comparative law at Rutgers Law School in New Jersey, USA, and later at Columbia Law School in New York City, USA, where she also taught constitutional law. In 1970 she co-founded the first US law journal to focus solely on women's rights, the *Women's Rights Law Reporter*. Two years later in

1972 she co-founded the Women's Rights Project at the American Civil Liberties Union (ACLU), later becoming one of the ACLU's general counsel. She argued six gender discrimination cases before the Supreme Court – five of which she won.

She was appointed a judge of the US Court of Appeals for the District of Columbia Circuit by President Jimmy Carter in 1980. In 1993, President Bill Clinton announced his nomination of Ginsburg to the Supreme Court. She was endorsed unanimously by the Senate Judiciary Committee, and confirmed by the full Senate by a vote of 96–3, making her only the second female justice of four to be confirmed to the court.

Throughout her legal career Ginsburg has advocated for women's rights and social equality. She has authored numerous landmark decisions, including *United States v. Virginia*, in which the Supreme Court declared unconstitutional the long-standing male-only policy of the Virginia Military Institute. Another prominent case, *Olmstead v. L.C.*, recognized mental illness as a form of disability, thus enabling it to be covered under the Americans with Disabilities Act. She is also considered to have been instrumental in the Supreme Court's historic decision in the *Obergefell v. Hodges* case that made same-sex marriage legal in all fifty states of the USA.

In 2010, after fifty-six years of marriage, Marty Ginsburg passed away from complications related to metastatic cancer. He first battled with cancer in Jane's infancy, when he was diagnosed with testicular cancer. Ginsburg described Marty as her biggest booster, and 'the only young man I dated who cared that I had a brain.'[11] The day after his death, she announced an opinion at the Court because, 'it was what he would have wanted'.[12]

Ginsburg's outspokenness has inspired numerous pop-culture references, including a Tumblr blog created by a second-year law student at New York University entitled "Notorious R.B.G." – a play on the stage name of American rapper "Notorious B.I.G". In 2016, Ginsburg released a collection of her writings, *My Own Words*, which became a *New York Times* bestseller. In 2018 CNN Films released a documentary about Ginsburg titled *RBG*, which received one BAFTA, two Academy Award and four Emmy nominations. Another film, *On the Basis of Sex*, was also released later in 2018, starring Felicity Jones as Ginsburg.

Ginsburg is the recipient of various awards and recognitions, including a Thurgood Marshall Award for contributions to gender equality and civil rights, and honorary Doctor of Laws degrees from numerous universities, including Harvard, Yale, Princeton, Columbia, and the University of Lund in Sweden. She was inducted into the National Women's Hall of Fame in 2002, named on the *Forbes* list of "The World's 100 Most Powerful Women" in 2004, and *Time* magazine's 2015 list of the "100 Most Influential People in the World".

About the Project

'A true leader must work hard to ease tensions, especially when dealing with sensitive and complicated issues. Extremists normally thrive when there is tension, and pure emotion tends to supersede rational thinking.'

– Nelson Mandela

Inspired by Nelson Mandela, *I Know This to Be True* was conceived to record and share what really matters for the most inspiring leaders of our time.

I Know This to Be True is a Nelson Mandela Foundation project anchored by original interviews with twelve different and extraordinary leaders each year, for five years – six men and six women – who are helping and inspiring others through their ideas, values and work.

Royalties from sales of this book will support language translation and free access to films, books and educational programmes using material from the series, in all countries with developing economies, or economies in transition, as defined by United Nations annual classifications.

iknowthistobetrue.org

'A good head and a good
heart are always a formidable
combination.'

– Nelson Mandela

A special thanks to Ruth Bader Ginsburg, and all the generous and inspiring individuals we call leaders who have magnanimously given their time to be part of this project.

For the Nelson Mandela Foundation:
Sello Hatang, Verne Harris, Noreen Wahono,
Razia Saleh and Sahm Venter

For Blackwell & Ruth:
Geoff Blackwell, Ruth Hobday, Cameron Gibb,
Nikki Addison, Olivia van Velthooven, Elizabeth Blackwell,
Kate Raven, Annie Cai and Tony Coombe

We hope that together we can help to mobilize Madiba's extraordinary legacy, to the benefit of communities around the world.

A note from the photographer
The photographic portraits in this book are the result of a team effort, led by Blackwell & Ruth's talented design director Cameron Gibb, who both mentored and saved this fledgling photographer. I have long harboured the desire, perhaps conceit, that I could personally create photographs for one of our projects, but through many trials, and more than a few errors, I learned that without Cameron's generous direction and sensitivity, I couldn't have come close to creating these portraits. I would also like to acknowledge the on-the-ground support of John Boal for helping me capture these images of Ruth Bader Ginsburg.

– Geoff Blackwell

About Nelson Mandela

Nelson Mandela was born in the Transkei, South Africa, on 18 July 1918. He joined the African National Congress in the early 1940s and was engaged in struggles against the ruling National Party's apartheid system for many years before being arrested in August 1962. Mandela was incarcerated for more than twenty-seven years, during which his reputation as a potent symbol of resistance for the anti-apartheid movement grew steadily. Released from prison in 1990, Mandela was jointly awarded the Nobel Peace Prize in 1993, and became South Africa's first democratically elected president in 1994. He died on 5 December 2013, at the age of ninety-five.

NELSON MANDELA
FOUNDATION
Living the legacy

About the Nelson Mandela Foundation

The Nelson Mandela Foundation is a non-profit organization founded by Nelson Mandela in 1999 as his post-presidential office. In 2007 he gave it a mandate to promote social justice through dialogue and memory work.

Its mission is to contribute to the making of a just society by mobilizing the legacy of Nelson Mandela, providing public access to information on his life and times and convening dialogue on critical social issues.

The Foundation strives to weave leadership development into all aspects of its work.

nelsonmandela.org

Notes and Sources

i   The Second Red Scare, widely known as 'McCarthyism' during the period after World War II (1939–45). A heightened popular fear of communist espionage as a result of various international events including the Soviet occupation of Eastern Europe, the Berlin Blockade (1948–49), the end of the Chinese Civil War, confessions of Soviet espionage by several high-ranking US government officials, and the outbreak of the Korean War.

ii   Thurgood Marshall (1908–93), American lawyer and first African-American Associate Justice of the US Supreme Court, from 1967 to 1991. Successfully argued several cases before the Supreme Court, including *Brown v. Board of Education*.

iii   Amelia Mary Earhart (b. 1897, disappeared on 2 July 1937 in the Pacific Ocean and declared dead in absentia on 5 January 1939), American aviation pioneer and author. First female aviator to fly solo across the Atlantic Ocean.

iv   Nancy Drew is a fictional American character who first appeared in 1930 in a mystery fiction series for young adults. Created by publisher Edward Stratemeyer as the female counterpart to *The Hardy Boys* series and published under the pseudonym Carolyn Keene.

v   The Second Red Scare, also known as 'McCarthyism'.

vi   House Un-American Activities Committee (HUAC) (also called the House Committee on Un-American Activities [HCUA]). Investigative committee of the US House of Representatives created in 1938 to investigate alleged disloyalty and subversive activities by private citizens, public employees, and organizations suspected of having Communist ties.

vii   The HUAC's anti-communist investigations are often compared with those of US Senator Joseph McCarthy, but he had no direct involvement with HUAC – he was the chairman of the Government Operations Committee and its Permanent Subcommittee on Investigations of the US Senate.

viii   A term used to describe a young woman who attends college or university with the intention of finding a potential spouse.

ix   John Paul Stevens (1920–2019), American lawyer, jurist and associate justice of the US Supreme Court from 1975 until 2010.

x   Paraphrasing Alexis Charles-Henri-Maurice Clérel, Viscount de
     Tocqueville (1805–59), French diplomat, political scientist, historian
     and author of *Democracy in America*. Tocqueville observed "The
     greatness of America lies not in being more enlightened than any
     other nation, but rather in her ability to repair her faults."

xi   Billings Learned Hand (1872–1961), American judge, served on the US
     District Court for the Southern District of New York and the US Court
     of Appeals for the Second Circuit.

1   Geoff Blackwell and Ruth Hobday, *200 Women: Who Will Change the Way You See the World* (San Francisco, USA: Chronicle Books, 2017), p. 224.

2   Ibid.

3   Abbe R. Gluck and Gillian Metzger, "A Conversation with Justice Ruth Bader Ginsburg" (2013), Faculty Scholarship Series, *Yale Law School Legal Scholarship Repository*", p. 9, https://digitalcommons.law.yale.edu/fss_papers/4905.

4   Ibid, p. 29.

5   Jeffrey Rosen, "Ruth Bader Ginsburg Opens Up About #MeToo, Voting Rights, and Millennials", *The Atlantic*, 15 February 2018, https://www.theatlantic.com/politics/archive/2018/02/ruth-bader-ginsburg-opens-up-about-metoo-voting-rights-and-millenials/553409/.

6   *Frontiero v. Richardson* (No. 71-1694), 1973.

7   Thurgood Marshall, "Remarks of Thurgood Marshall at the Annual Seminar of the San Francisco Patent and Trademark Law Association", Maui, Hawaii, USA, 6 May 1987, http://thurgoodmarshall.com/the-bicentennial-speech/.

8   *The RBG Workout: How She Stays Strong – and You Can Too!*, Bryant Johnson (Boston, USA: Houghton Mifflin Harcourt Publishing Company, 2017).

9   *Frontiero v. Richardson* (No. 71-1694), 1973.

10   Paraphrased from Judge Learned Hand's "The Spirit of Liberty" speech, May 1944, I AM an American Day (now Citizenship Day).

11   Geoff Blackwell and Ruth Hobday, *200 Women: Who Will Change the Way You See the World* (San Francisco, USA: Chronicle Books, 2017), p. 224.

12   Brian P. Smentkowski and Aaron M. Houck, Encyclopedia Britannica, "Ruth Bader Ginsburg", https://www.britannica.com/biography/Ruth-Bader-Ginsburg.

Permissions

The publisher is grateful for literary permissions to reproduce items subject to copyright which have been used with permission. Every effort has been made to trace the copyright holders and the publisher apologizes for any unintentional omission. We would be pleased to hear from any not acknowledged here and undertake to make all reasonable efforts to include the appropriate acknowledgement in any subsequent edition.

Pages 6, 11, 12, 21, 26: *200 Women: Who Will Change the Way You See the World* (Chronicle Books: San Francisco, USA, 2017), copyright © 2017 Blackwell and Ruth Limited; pages 13, 14–15, 44, 49: "A Conversation with Justice Ruth Bader Ginsburg", Abbe R. Gluck and Gillian Metzger, *Faculty Scholarship Series*, 2013, digitalcommons.law.yale.edu/fss_papers/4905; page 15: "Ruth Bader Ginsburg Opens Up About #MeToo, Voting Rights, and Millennials", © 2018 Jeffrey Rosen, as first published in *The Atlantic*, theatlantic.com/politics/archive/2018/02/ruth-baderginsburg-opens-up-about-metoo-voting-rights-and-millenials/553409; pages 19–20: "University of Buffalo Honorary Degree Remarks", Amherst, New York, USA, 26 August 2019; page 33: Julie Cohen and Betsy West, *RBG*, 2018; page 41: "A Conversation with Justice Ruth Bader Ginsburg", *The Record*, 56, issue no. 1 (Winter 2001): pages 9–22, reprinted with permission of the New York City Bar Association; page 54: "Honoring Ruth Bader Ginsburg", Colleen Walsh, *The Harvard Gazette*, 29 May 2015, news.harvard.edu/gazette/story/2015/05/honoring-ruth-bader-ginsburg; pages 59–60: "Remarks at the New York Historical Society", New-York Historical Society, 10 April 2018; page 61: Irin Carmon and Shana Knizhnik, *Notorious RBG: The Life and Times of Ruth Bader Ginsburg* (Dey Street Books, an imprint and division of HarperCollins, New York, USA, 2015); pages 67–68: *Nelson Mandela by Himself: The Authorised Book of Quotations* edited by Sello Hatang and Sahm Venter (Pan Macmillan: Johannesburg, South Africa, 2017), copyright © 2011 Nelson R. Mandela and the Nelson Mandela Foundation, used by permission of the Nelson Mandela Foundation, Johannesburg, South Africa.

First published in the United States of America in 2020 by Chronicle Books LLC.

Produced and originated by
Blackwell and Ruth Limited
Suite 405, Ironbank,150 Karangahape Road
Auckland 1010, New Zealand
www.blackwellandruth.com

Publisher: Geoff Blackwell
Editor in Chief & Project Editor: Ruth Hobday
Design Director: Cameron Gibb
Designer & Production Coordinator: Olivia van Velthooven
Publishing Manager: Nikki Addison
Digital Publishing Manager: Elizabeth Blackwell

Images copyright © 2020 Geoff Blackwell
Layout and design copyright © 2020 Blackwell and Ruth Limited
Introduction by Nikki Addison

Acknowledgements for permission to reprint previously published
and unpublished material can be found on page 79. All other text
copyright © 2020 Blackwell and Ruth Limited.

Library of Congress Cataloging-in-Publication Data available.

ISBN 978-1-7972-0016-3

Chronicle Books LLC
680 Second Street
San Francisco, CA 94107
www.chroniclebooks.com

10 9 8 7 6 5 4 3 2 1

Manufactured in China by 1010 Printing Ltd.